# freedomland blues

henry 7. reneau, jr.

Transcendent Zero Press

Houston, TX

Copyright © 2014 henry 7. reneau, jr.

PUBLISHED BY TRANSCENDENT ZERO PRESS
*www.transcendentzeropress.org*

All rights reserved. No part or parts of this book may be reproduced in any format without the expressed written consent of Transcendent Zero Press, or of the author henry 7. reneau, jr.

ISBN-13: 978-0-6923911-1-2
ISBN-10: 0-692391118
Library of Congress Control Number: 2015933944

Printed in the United States of America

16429 El Camino Real Apt. 7
Houston, TX 77062

Cover Design: AJ Price Design

SECOND EDITION
Transcendent Zero Press

for Agnes Philomena Wade Reneau

*. . . singing freedom songs the color of love*

# CONTENTS

blind hope blues     [1]

**1.**

red     [3]

match & gasoline blues     [4]

reflecting Yahweh #2     [6]

eyes shut wide: in response to every cowardly, self-serving Amerikkkan poet who has taken a hands-off approach to every disturbing reality . . .     [7]

Democracy     [9]

security, in progress     [10]

watch what they mouth say & listen what they hands do     [12]

intervention per serendipity     [14]

selective recall     [16]

the anxiety blues     [18]

Sigourney Valentine O'Connell, aka Muse     [19]

seven days in oz     [21]

dissent relegated to the annuls of history     [22]

the terminal blues     [23]

tradition     [24]

bitter margins     [26]

physiography of the fittest     [27]

blanket-stash red, white & blues     [29]

chrysalises     [31]

Max Goes to Buy a Goldfish     [32]

agápe     [34]

**2.**

the price of flight     [36]

fattening frogs for king snakes     [38]

The Lion Pauses     [39]

allotment     [40]

the soul would have no rainbow if eyes had no tears     [42]

Requiem for Eve: A Whiter Shade of Pale in Five Parts     [43]

I Aim to Misbehave!     [44]

I Am Trayvon Martin!     [48]

damaged goods     [50]

the famous-for-being-famous blues     [51]

stranger than fiction     [53]

comeuppance: the self-serving     [55]

the salvage blues     [56]

SEPT. 11:
cheney's puppet seizes 31$^{st}$ piece of silver     [58]

Eve #2     [60]

broke-ass blues     [61]

Chance is what's left, when you've run out of hope.     [63]

synonym the low bass quiver     [64]

El-Hajj Malik El-Shabazz     [65]

waste is everything nobody needs     [67]

fade to black     [68]

*Acknowledgements*     [69]

## blind hope blues

**for trena riley**

the blues toil within a gilded, circular vacuum.
when the Mason jar tilt sideways
                         hobbled lightening bugs
illuminate the world inside their glass cage
with their last remaining light,
beauty within emptiness,
                         like an eclipse of the sun,
hidden in plain sight.

we are witness
& commotion is the atmosphere we swim in.

the blues toil within a brick-walled,
                         linear vacuum
that takes more than Elvis to fill.     frustration
stutter-steps, a heartbeat
                         across a horizon-less plane
where God & the Devil circle in pugilism,
like ancient, rusting cars idling in tall grass,
beauty within emptiness,
                         hidden in plain sight.

# 1.

the Blues: beautiful as the resistance we are shaped against, like
    an animal thought dead suddenly scrabbling to its feet.

**red**

for sabrina macias, on lock-down

a caution shade of combustion all appetite:
Revlon red lipstick that mimics
arousal & pornographic, vermilion fingernails
accentuate a splayed erotic;

red hair kissed by flaming fire
to sensual awakening, Ann-Margret's purr,
a perfect flint to start a quarrel, or bullet
that portends a war;

fist-tight crimson resurrected & flung
into scorching solar wind,
white phosphorous phoenix, all molten red
& gold immolation

& frightened russet sparrows
running red-light scared
& brushfire sweep of abandon-ship crows
launch into arsonist auburn sky

before an obsession with the pyre, terror-blind
terrific as all Creation.    ascending angel-ablaze
& dancing as Divine, a red rebellious heart
enflamed & rising from the stake, to cardinal
conflagration,

to red-shift reincarnation
at the igneous end of panic, scarlet obsession
to vaporization,
to crematoria bone-gray ash & reborn
an unrequited, yet intimate, act of passion.

**match & gasoline blues**

everything starts somewhere,
                              in legend that begins with longing
deep & wide as Jim Crow's swallow,     from a place inside
that has no name.                      begins in plantation lullaby
& church house choir.     in cotton field holla' &
up-country jook-joint blues, as white-sheeted crows
                                        climb from the bushes.
from the guv'ment.     as chain-gang boss-man.
longing takes a leap of faith, begins a journey from desperation—
a compass fashioned from hope & willful apprehension—
like put-the-hammer-down
pushin' a Cadillac named desire,     giddy with dreams
unseated from the hollow about the heart.     over the wall, to flee,
searching like the mad
              for a gap in tribulation, between sorrow song & alone.
it plucks "shave & a haircut, six bits" from cat-gut & wood,
seeking danger that has a rhythm,     sex that has a sound
                        & freedom with a music all its own.

everything starts somewhere,
         with what *the men don't know, but the little girls understand,*
why, the first time a girl took off her drawers     & threw them on the stage,
they called that the blues.
why, when white girls started doing it, they called it rock & roll.     legend
writ large in blackbirds of shadow,
                              veering from a telephone line
omen of crows, a corvid rising & falling
through haloes of carrion urgency,

to spontaneous combustion bad as Superman—
                         Mississippi come to Memphis,
come to Chi-town howlin' at the moon, a bullet,
                  come in Sunday suit & star-sequined socks,
come in trademark hat—with somebody else's name—
         like holy roller scripture come to burn the house down.

Son House & Muddy Waters,                    Howlin' Wolf &
John Lee Hooker.    straight razor voice raising Calvary to salvation,
spiritual uplift after sorrow—     misery, knife-cuttin' the gunslinger-

six-string appendage of road-hardened ax,   a backwoods wail
of take-me-to-chu'ch! Blues-man harp   & methamphetamine piano
tweakin' ivory keys of black & blue to mortal redemption:
                              eviscerate the narrative,
read it backwards like gospel & make it explode.
got that John tha' Conquer root,
                  Johnnie Walker & they mojo workin' too.

& everybody start to sing,    a jook-joint jubilation that cancels every sin.

**Note:** song lyric fragment by Howlin' Wolf, from "Back Door Man"

## reflecting Yahweh #2

*. . . say my name, & every color illumines*
—Florence + the Machine

the human soul
carries the scent of things lost in the fire,
the magnetic nostalgia
of good times & our life once folded inward
by ill circumstance,
to hindsight,
into the effusive syntax of memory
like the aperture to a captured moment in time,
an instant of eternity
with the stealth of a broken promise

**eyes shut wide: in response to every cowardly, self-serving Amerikkkan poet who has taken a hands-off approach to every disturbing reality . . .**

maybe, i should write a poem
about the twelve-year old who committed suicide,
the future cure for democracy, now muted silence,
hanging from a rafter in his bedroom of Amerikkka,
while blue-blood silver spoons tucked in tight &
sweet buzzed on prescription meds
despite it's open season
on them who are least of those among us.

maybe, i should write a poem about Etan Patz',
the six-year old who vanished
on the first day
he was allowed to walk to school alone     & became
among the first vanished children
to appear on a milk carton;
maybe that would bring
some level of closure to the parents—
unlike poets contemplating rays of sunlight illuminating window blinds,
as they explicate the landscape of their lover's thighs, out of synch
with the precarious tilt of Amerikkkan life.

or the county dump seagull, squawking away,
persisting
at the meager hint of a crumb
amongst scraps of technology, concrete &
millions of plastic bottles—
his whole life spent never having seen the sea,
weened on the fossil fuel of mammoth dozers sifting human waste,
that reeks of *gimme' more!*, & not so much, we've taken more
than everything we need.

or innocence,
that teaches what it feels like to be used,
a beggar's empty cup, the sweet dreams
made of anything that gets us seen—
en-flocked—despite the dangling noose in every tree
like the polluted air of thorns we breathe.

maybe i should write a poem
about five-year old Ella, who imagines my "fixie" bike
as an earring heirloom chained to a tree, colorful & chrome-bright;
or seven-year old W. James,
who can only envision a game of marbles
as a kaleidoscope of stars, their flash & sparkle of pinball chance colliding
inside a circular galaxy, inside a circumference
of plausible deniability that children just can't see—their tiny hands
clasped in optimistic prayers of make believe salvation—children
filling soon darkening spaces with imagination, with the meaningless plea:
*now i lay me down to sleep . . .*

**Note:** Among the first vanished children (1979) to appear on a milk carton, Etan Patz' became a symbol of a movement to draw attention to child safety. The day of his disappearance, May 25, became National Missing Children's Day. The case bedeviled investigators as leads emerged and fizzled over the years; Etan, never found, was officially declared dead in 2001.

**Democracy**

  after Carl Adamshick

We took the shirt off your back & in a few days
  you'll see we tracked your cell-phone GPS, your credit card.

We've devised a new identity.

We've conspired, taken photos & fingerprints. We took the photos & the prints.

We took your first born, your parental rights.
We took your home & watched
  as dignity fell from you.

We took your freedom,
  sewed it on our sleeves
  & flaunted it before you
  as just another thing we've granted selectively, or withheld.

**security, in progress**

the echo of an echo of inaction
sickle &
whetstone-like turned cheek
of Jesus Christ
& collateral damage in progress
as imminent
dire as Bogie's now famous snarl &
lisp as menacing
as 16 seconds between
the trigger pulled in Las Vegas &
        the Hellfire missile landing
in Pakistan, after which
they ask: did we hit a child?      no
        a wedding procession?!
& always    we
hold these truths to be self-evidence
of post-9/11    rules of engagement
(obey
      consume   conform &
                        breed
             watch t.v.
    lies are truth
stay very afraid
        war is peace &
                black is bad)
a metallic flavor
contaminating most of the air
as she drove two blocks to the 7/11
for a low-fat
chemical-ful of excito-toxic
micro-waved burrito
& a Big Gulp
of corn-syrup cloyingly sweet
                Coca-Cola
& 20 newborn babies
keeled over dead
from upper respiratory distress
irregardless of the insomniac
stepped outside

                    to smoke a cigarette
safely removed
20 ft. from every public entrance

**watch what they mouth say & listen
what they hands do**

i grew up hearing certain accents
& vocabularies
& speech patterns
that were the aural essence of H*ome*
or the audible signal of danger.

only acceptance has taken hold, a feral howl
of an indifferent way
to make *Home* a muted whisper of fear, painful
& slow to change, that is now, & maybe, then,
like a metaphor that reflects how it ought to be,
trying to reach the next world
with a spoon,
(*thrust    lever    lift    toss*)

a soundtrack of false platitudes
painting the air of thorns about my ears,
continually looping a distorted truth
as pragmatic symbolism for freedom,
as a gimp
would drag the weight of her body.

the mute icon depressed: a deleted
allotment of common sense:
blind, cripple & crazy as a
long aching silence
in which we hear nothing
but the clean crack of hearts breaking
& the accepted ruin
of *matters of fact*,
a shovel, searching out the truth,
*(thrust    lever    lift    toss)*

a soundtrack now,
painting funeral dirges
of carrion eagles & securitized oil,
& the façade of propaganda:
an Oscar worthy suspension of disbelief

showcasing the murder of bin Laden,
that goes viral & seals a book deal,
& movie credits for Seal Team 6,
*(thrust    lever    lift    toss).*

**intervention per serendipity**

streamlined in asphalt-covered glamour
there's no pattern
to this upwardly-mobile repetition,
     as i calculate the variables
         in chasing success like a quota
& the tedium
as i merge into gridlock,
drive-at-five isolation: conditioned frigid-aire & i-pod
50 watts per channel on damn-near mute
     because the pace of life is moving way too fast,
    a mechanized metal through molten air,
to unexpected impolitic,
as onrushing serendipity,
to road rage bears its ugly face when some asshole cuts me off &
flings the universal abbreviation
      of indifference—
a middle-finger fuck you!—from the driver's side window.
my gorilla shifts for better purchase,
slams
into the gilded bars of its civilized cage
    under a suddenly
    atom bomb-emblazoned,
premonition sky:
    rainbow red & blueyellowgreen,
         threat-level orange,
cathedral-domed across eight lanes
& Barry White elevator muzak
sound-tracked, as angels appear    onetwothreefourfive,
    clad in wife beaters &
    GAP red-bead-for-Africa straight-fit khakis.
then,
from the oleander median strip,
burning bush-like, suddenly explodes
     a runaway detonation
     of megaton Mack truck,
regurgitating comeuppance as a Divine elimination,
    dancing around the conscripted ignorant,
     drunks & privileged children,
      to find the fool.

breaking news flash: sole survivor in 15 car pile-up
                                        saved by jaws of life . . . except
                                                                         for his middle finger.

**selective recall**

**we don't see things as they are; we see them as we are**
                                            **-Anaïs Nin**

i remember my daughter's first smile
beneath a maternity ward micky d heating lamp
recall as hauntingly familiar as battery acid
thrown into a public pool filled with black children

i remember wearing levi 501s
raybans
black panther/huelga/power to the people! buttons
to my high school graduation
& the echo of a gunshot as the messiah fell to hate

i remember first love's
tentative carousing puppy love
an emotion so deep i almost perished
like the soldier flogged lynched & castrated
on the soil he fought to save
hand to heart pledging red whiter blue(s)

i remember signs leading disciplined anger
*i am a man!*
rocks & bottles flying
&
scalding words like rock salt in open wounds
&
ill-mannered fire hose pushing & shoving
men women & children
&
snarling gestapo hounds keyed on hate

i remember . . .
chewy the pimp at the main motel on union ave.
*to live life, you take the bitter with the sweet*

i remember . . .
that ear-ringin' beam-me-up boo-yah sizzle
as the gorilla shifted
for better purchase on my back
i remember . . .
things were better yesterday that weren't

**the anxiety blues**

the harmonica's fearful wail
an ascending shriek of looming prophecy, not smoke
but the space
inside a rectangle of vacuum
that hungers
to be filled
sluicing away breath
to suspend the hiss
of apprehension scratched haphazard
into our skin
not one choice     but hundreds
not one trap
but hundreds & hundreds
until we do not even feel it &
always
someone else's misery
in everything we need to want
always
there is more than enough
of everything
filling the world with obsession
with toothless particles
made from the everything of me, mine & more
the hesitant touch between strangers
reading foreign into first impressions
into more elastic, ingrained terrorism
for which we each have to find
our own courage
sometimes beckoning benediction
blossoming birds-of-paradise, red-tongued & speared
sometimes happiness incognito
the horse that moves backwards
as we face forward     complex colliding
of cell-phones ringing off the hook
as dissonance that distances, but simultaneously
attracts
the elongated substance of our fear
an exhalation of breath that hungers to be filled

## Sigourney Valentine O'Connell, aka Muse

Sigourney, aka Ziggy, muse of my dreams to me,
conjures a pipe wrench from my tongue

to tighten aerodynamic sounds:
ashes to ashes, dust to dust

congealed to flat rocks skimming water,
airborne as a singular adjective.

her eyes, emerald green to blue flint & spark,
to hazel tint that inspires me,

filling my mind with epiphany,
to eat from bowls: mouthfuls of sound,

consonants garnish vowels
with a bright light vision

now revealed as inner eye &
rested on a sheltered, park bench,

wind against my face
& long shadows at my back.

feminine singular, she spins a spell
rising bad tidings from Obeah's mouth,

from endless curve of ass & thigh
handcuffed to the bedpost with elastic words,

from jagged depth of wanton greed,
from as-the-crow-flies;

her moral parallel questions
& challenges the machine.

Muse: hot, groaning station
from which train cars issue,

unraveling to rhymes that shape her,
& keep on moving—magic, long as train smoke.

**seven days in oz**

smilin' like a shark in a bloodbank
time slows
in grains-of-sand increments
distilling wonder & planning frayed

like broken threads
in the machined tapestry of life &
moral debt for things we didn't do
when we should have did
congeal to the blood-red elixir of guilt

the heart tick-tocks a stutter-step beat
counting existence one penny at a time &
growin' into the grave

the past accumulates to death
out of synch with struggle, bleeding hope
from the music of ordinary life

## dissent relegated to the annuls of history

society lives an arm's-length between us
forged wrathful as counterfeit
despite politic mumblings
of cogs & parroting

false platitudes
like long-distance machine-tooled force
making them round, notched & oily
like the artificial, rouged ember of a whore

willing to do anything to tell the world everything
like the end of a cigarette burning against the night

will produce a subconscious sense of violence
like a loaded nine millimeter
& the tenacity of bullets

an incremental shudder to a full stop
where there are only two or three human stories
to dissipate shadows within words & illuminate silence

i know something ugly is coming
an indifference like a machine that mimics silence
& unspoken slights
where stars make outside brighter
than without
a voice

## the terminal blues

a journey begun eager to reach a final destination: the nest
left bare & dangling,
emptied & without as tear-stained goodbyes—
as dust,
the light burned out &
drifted
beyond the gravity of its luminance,
departure as anxious flow, no, more like a faucet's slow drip,
bleeding from an extremity & needing
the grip of a wrench
to stem the forever mortal losses.

the expanse of time, as keen of scouring wind, slamming
the door closed,
as a window opens into all that is possible,
something enormous
that flicks a tobacco-stained tongue.     from in the beginning
the end is near,
weighted down with toppled palms & broken glass,
with whip rain torrent of tears &
shattered windshields scattered diamonds in the road,
with feral breath capriciously blown into an empty bottle—
with the burden of Atlas, which we carry
on our backs.

destiny-like destination, sliding down while holding on-
to a crumbling horizon: a moment of sun
between squalls of rain that smell of violets, tombstones & ash,
that which happens, instead
of the other way around,
as the tide rises & compels us all
toward the frigid, blue lip of some possibly dreadful new world.

**tradition**

this story's validity is intensified by the number of generations it took
to reach here;

this story, about prolonged suffering:
a stand of pink flamingos starving on nuclear-brown suburban lawns
grown sterile as the dissenting clamor          of children's voices
beyond the yellowed margins of obituaries
& submissive prayer
reduced to whispered words after suffering—a couple of lines
stitched onto tribulation, like a long wait for a train don't come

during those moments
when we fled to the cliff's edge          & exhaled
& always, everything we do ends up empty, a three-day-old sweat of
                                                              frustration,
dis-remembering an equatorial sweetness pushing through our veins
& a Middle Passage on the horizon,
portending all the myriad horrors one should never see

—*like Jesus walking the Blues is how we once knew black,*

the cogs, wheels & spindles of a great manipulated dynamic—
the life of things now given over to an economic disparity practiced as
religion, & *less than*
rationalized by the clinical calculations of academia,

a keening sound
spinning federal-green dreams of Freedomland,          an irradiation,
silently purring blind hope on stealthy feline feet,   a nocturnal stalker,
as in, heathen sinner born again to suffer now-greater later

—the missing shade, a lily-white variable that niggers a personality,
breeding architects of our own self-destruction—
& the headlines read:
ICE-BOX KILLER CLAIMS EIGHTH

& here come 5-0 gangbangers under color of long-arm Johnny Law,
a thin blue line between ballin' & 25 to life,     roamin' ghetto streets,
circlin' the block, searchin' my niggas' inside out,        pullin' nines

& knots
out they pockets & they socks, findin' dope,        the concealed Glock,
whether theirs or not—
                    as uptown white collar dumps ninth in vacant lot

# bitter margins

### abandon all hope, all ye who enter here

looking for someone who is supposed to exist,
                                                  but nobody's seen,

someone who's already dead
& swooping down silent.
                              there are so many of us incog-negro,

mesmerized by the sounds that mimic
a post-racial gathering under twilight skies, betrayed by hope

& patronizing our plummet with "better than it used to be"
as we distill into the shadow of echo & soundlessly

floating; a last witness amidst the debris of desperation,
mouths scarred shut
                   by the bitter awfulness of living in the margins

& blood coloring the air thickened by frustration,
amassed; struggling from the hem            into starlight.

sputtering flame unfolding, becoming grace set free &
beating the air above a moonlit surge of sea—

the farther shore a distant anguish of nearness—
mirroring a silent desire, a phantom ache

of amputated dreams within the Veil;         a paranoia
as intimate as sin after the careen of silence & too many tears

through too many years.      i know just how that onion feel,
all wrapped tight,           mummified rage awaiting release.

## physiography of the fittest

1.

a swarm
the horde
that descends
depicting
a predator
by its proper
plural
a lynch mob
the murder

2.

an Aztec
pyramid
guilt-ridden
by human sacrifice
as it capitulates
to the scorpions
scuttling across
its crumbling
steps

3.

eons of heat &
pressure compressed
the smudge
of coal
to diamond
brilliance
beneath the
rapacious
burden of progress

4.

the .45 cal.
patriarchy of Adam's
blue-steel arrogance
in the face of
feminine resolve with
the last handful of bullets

## blanket-stash red, white & blues

> . . . the errand boy sent by grocery clerks
> to collect the bill.
> —"Apocalypse Now"

flies amassed
about the enemy's spilled guts
come & see, the pale green horse
rocket apogee of death
& the high angle of hell
hath followed with him
who once believed
Amerikkka was God &
country worth dying for, but
from where
he now panhandles
it stinks of expendable &
mechanical police-goon threats
parroting "quality of life" commands:
*don't be here when we come back!*

escaped unscathed
from the rabid mouth of madness
defined: complicit in
pre-emptive war &
come home to
demon frost winter
gripped the homeless vet by the throat
after two tours fighting terrorism &
taught to believe
what he was ordered to believe
fighting for "freedom & democracy"

returned the traumatized hero
defined: *not economically viable*
sing-song mumbled
the homeless vet
a cardboard sign in hand: will kill
for loose change

for work, a roof overhead
a malt liquor "forty" to forget—
a cigarette

his once patriotic dogma
enacting massacres in our name
a warrior mind animated
by exploding ghosts
of the foreign horde:
men, women &
the children—their faces
shredded to collateral damage
the innocent
always the least able
to dive for cover
when drones co-sign propaganda
as national security &
his remorse in denial
like once-opened doors slamming
& his heart-stutter PTSD
as all of a sudden as vipers
war-makers & profiteers
like instinctive murder
that has a voice
a blood-stained, metallic-copper
guilt
after promises
that have not been kept
after honor bought &
paid for
with Amerikkkan tax dollars
one ragtag nation under God
now turned to slow suicide &
we bury the dead alive
in Salvation Army soup lines &
rain-soaked cardboard boxes

**chrysalises**

ambition in chains, a nineteenth-century dream of freedom

marking time in an expanding universe.     a galaxy of dust
awakened from the stasis of anxiety & shouts its free will.

transient sediment of cyclical immortality: a vagrant dream
of perambulation in shards of fallen leaves, moisture   & rot.

a song comes to mind & Adam throws off the yoke,
cocks an opposable thumb into a selective weapon of war &

drought thirsty, mistletoe strangled, gravity-compelled limbs
assume a patient reincarnation, reborn

as smudges of coal, evincing moments of compressed clarity
ringing true as diamonds              & life is more than

mute perishing, an elemental, in the waiting, for awakening.

# Max Goes to Buy a Goldfish

**for Dr. Andy Jones, storyteller**

Max goes to buy a goldfish.

He finds himself
traveling further into an illustrated book
by way of imagination,
along the yellow brick road
of fairy tale.

Once upon a time . . .
(breadcrumbs optional)
far into an arboreal maze
of fern & gully,
babbling brooks in shady glens
accompanied by
the intermittent chorus
of the unfamiliar made fearsome:
haunting birdcalls,
cryptic trills & lonesome howls of hunger
that began
with a bus ride to the pet shop,
that began with a Yolo bus transfer &
an impromptu conversation
with a gifted storyteller—
a Dr. Andy—
relating a "Truman-ism,"
a guilelessness
in colors so bright
it could only have come from a child's imagination:
*No, we're not gonna' kill mommy, because I need an assistant . . .*
providing filler to drive the plot.

Max soon realizes he is hitchhiking from a dead-end life,
diverted from the dusty trail
by the possibility of the impossible
that comes shaped
so he can live inside a song:
stanzas of multi-colored tulips
rising from snowed-in slumber

to beckoning sunshine.

His wonder & awe
now thick as imagination in triumph,
laughing & beating the dust from his clothes,
tasting dust inside his laughter,
as he leaves black & white monochrome
to begin his audacity-to-hope
in a Technicolor, Sen-surround world.

Always, everything we take
has to come from someplace else: always, the taken &
the given.

Once upon a time is the story of a boy,
the from-rags-to-riches via lottery luck,
evil stepmother
finally fed to the wolves &
shorn of Power of Attorney,
the jackhammer
to remove shining sword from ancient stone.

Sure, you've heard that one,
the pauper who becomes the confident Casanova:
arm-in-arm with star-candy
that resembles Scarlett Johansson
(she of the bangin' booty like a sistuh)
as they star-glide down the red carpet,
prince-like & princess-ly,
& he,
with a Jake Elwood suitcase full
of childlike wonder & awe,
carrying one empty fishbowl of hope.

**agápe**

**for Nicole "Nikky" Clesi**

i feel, therefore i am free
to more than mere exist
embrace my dreams &
        optimistic live
*cogito ergo sum*
my life as i see fit
in harmony with
i think, therefore i am
too wide-eyed all
awake to wonder &
unconditional love
that justifies alive
        my arms & legs
in levitation
            with awe
awake my eyes,
contract my heartbeat &
expanding galaxy-like
as reciprocal symmetry
        the inner me
rising topmost
through the effluvium
            of life
is beauty by virtue
      of a constant love
measuring my existence

## 2.

dissent: an affinity for disobedience rising from the hem & laughing to keep from crying—a tried-my-las'-nerve one too many times.

**the price of flight**

winged beauty frozen in a dream of sunlight
pulling from all directions at once,
              capturing her perfectly     & opening her form
to imagination, the clarity of pixilation,
redemption floating free in a molting blur of feathers,
turned to snow & drifting through the signature of oxygen—
wispy cirrus-fluff, windblown
                from some distant-star landscape of her soul;
she glides over sand & rock,
        her descending, dark humanness an illumination
by virtue of being free
                & the song of her shadow
makes mountains preen iridescent colors & cracks
      the desert open to the dynamics of thermal uplift—
the sun & wind blended around a body
     that possesses an allusive mix of ambition & optimism
                                        —ascent,
                    framed wholly
by the beckoning air of the unknown.

immortal daughter of Icarus:
              *angel come down from heaven yesterday,*
fallen from an endless crescendo of dreams
              through good-time jazz & molten 2AM blues,
wings expanded to hold whatever still trembles—
still breathes & orbits asteroid-like—
                          19 million miles from the Son,
but closer than any other orbiting folly to a fault,
                where gravity follows laws
that have not yet been discovered,
that have not yet been written—
          a connection of zero, where all nothingness
or something-ness
comes closer to the all than the hollowness of faith.

                              heaven's blue,
wings of feather & candle wax,
                        the nostalgic price of flight,
alive                 in the hollow secret of her bones,
reborn, the repaired redemption of fly away far
                              & fly away fast.

**Note:** quoted song fragment by Jimi Hendrix

## fattening frogs for king snakes

**it was the voice of a desultory fragment
of speech now, talking about "state" and "union"
how darkness turns at the wrist**
                              —Anne Waldman

you who were finally deceived
to believe in anything
the continuance
of your ignorance the focus of
their governing, the audacity of
hope now ant-like rhetoric of vision, bath salt
dope & flesh-eating junkies, expedient
authority in the interest of
national security, N.S.A. data mines
as the legislated evil that rapes freedom, but
where is the voice
that questions authority?
why enduring war?   why oil-drenched
grasping bloody hands?   why biting off
more than i can chew, when my share is
disparate to yours?   why the child "Skittle-d"
by devil-hate?   why six women jurors
acquitting the watchman?   why standard
operating procedure as
protocol?   why healthy dialogue or
nonviolent dissent,
as opposed to "fuck tha' po-lice! & tha' 5-0 too"
& you never asking *where
am i being led?*   only one small begging voice
in the muzzled choir singing Mary
don't you weep
o chicken little dodging the sky is falling! o the fallen
towers of stormy Monday blue(s),
counter-clockwise documenting
the homicidal hypocrisies in our tiny
capitulation, en-cubicled in a corporate
capatalist Wal-Mart parking lot, the pedestal
too high & we're so afraid of heights
as we hold our spoonful of truth to be self-evident that
it's not all our fault, that is never quite enough

## The Lion Pauses

Sunday, February 21st—standing at the podium,
The Audubon Ballroom in Harlem—

Preachin' to the choir & pauses
In a moment between tick & tock, a déjà vu that hovered

Above a glimpse of repetition,
Epiphany that sowed sorrow in the stutter of his heart;

His blood recounts the iron weight of shackles
& a balmy ocean breeze soothing an equatorial shore,

The sound of whiplash striking flesh & shots ring out
Has happened all before—as in, Pandora's Box,

When freedom became the ephemeral dream
& hope, handled with a chain, inside a frozen scream

**allotment**

1.

existing within the accepted belief that tragedy only happens
to someone else—held at arm's length by a sense of invulnerability
—is a rabid denial refuting a lot of confinement that is tailor-made

& eventual, a clarion blast of warning
from a lumbering freight train, bitchin' & moanin' in annoying screeches
of metal on metal & grinding a polished patina of acceptance
onto the derailment of life;

a lot that is monotonous with repetition

like over & over again, like amen! hallelujah!
& speaking in tongues 'bout praise jesus! that shades a life
the cloned-gray apathy of the herd
with its original sin that throbs regret-filled remorse.

2.

blindness & mistake in denial seamed into tapestries of behavior déjà vu
& nostalgic good old days & acceptance of what you'll never accomplish,
in the time you have left,

a lot of plans spun in youth that unspool hourglass sand
through grasping fingers, mercury dreams, too little, too late
we realize the real trouble we're in: tick-tock time, sorrow & life.

3.

allotment: we end up with we only get what we give is what we deserve;

4.

a lot of camouflage taken on at middle age, that others recognize
when we look in the mirror & only see *ourselves* that we want to see—
misery is my name—apart from the entanglement of introspection;

a lot of imprisonment within invisibility, incarcerated behind fugitive memories
concealed in plain sight—when muscles moved faster than thought & sex
was the only agenda—a loaded sidearm wrapped in oilcloth,
each bullet a penis anticipating discharge.

## the soul would have no rainbow if eyes had no tears
### inde trae et lacrimae

an abandoned tricycle in perdition's driveway
of shattered tonka™ toys
and a wary luke skywalker™ action figure
screams a pained-etched calligraphy of flayed innocence
sticks and stones . . . and words
leave broken bones . . . and scarred souls
conjured from spite and covetous lust and malodorous malice
dimming the starlight of twinkle, twinkle childhood magic
and peter pan i-can-fly wonder wonderful
sullied, rusting knives slicing onion tears

beasts of burdened guilt and shame
like circling crows above bowed heads and averted eyes
that beg forgiveness and acceptance
as ancient lullabies deceive amidst wreck and ruin
here . . . discordia's neon cry of pain
brutalized to anger's armageddon-red
seems ever judgmental of all god's chillun'

bent beneath the malice of pedophilic whim
innocence lays sprawled over headless barbie™
and muted ken™
and a torn dog-eared yugio™ trading card
that teaches what it means to be used
childhood in retreat, coerced by extorted secrets
circling buzzards above the void of helplessness
that promises
gasping   murmuring   gnawing   whistling
pain

faceless extremities of anonymity
preached   teached   beaten
left alone with nothing
brooding beneath the leash of selfish misuse
and violent sexual lunacy
bleeding self-hate and despair into freedomland's new utopia
. . . until janie gets a gun
hence the anger and these tears

## Requiem for Eve: A Whiter Shade of Pale in Five Parts

**They sense from a small cold place they are not themselves ...**
**from *Perdition* by Sophie Sills**

1.

The name-sayer of things, her muted hands on strings
  she cannot see an arch where-through
                          gleams that untraveled world.

2.

Her father's daughter,
a worn, red scarf frames her face
                in silken borders of religious submission.

3.

Adam's ego, in fear of falling,
  subjugates a female's dignity behind the veil,
                             a sucked-clean rib.

4.

Beneath the burka, a woman in solitude,
luminescence within the howling chaos of clenched fists
              & stones thrown, no tempo but tremulous.

5.

Not all who wander end up lost, only exile
              that carries her everywhere, eventually,
                    nowhere soon, anywhere she wants.

## I Aim to Misbehave!

who can really know what anyone feels?

brave
hearts
fulla'
two-fisted
fight,
still the
lament-
ation &
feral roar
of
almost
in
the
sound
of a moan,
having
marched,
having
organized &
challenged
death,
been
shot at,
cussed at &
spit at,
been abandoned on rooftops
in the middle of
a devastating hurricane—
we know what
the Mason-
Dixon line
represents—
always recalcitrant seeds of dis-Union,
having
never
melted
into this,

or any
other,
country—always
segregated as
you must
refrain from
being here
after
sundown
& always
nothing to
redeem
the thirty-three shades of fade to black,
too soon martyred
angels
of melted
wings
of wax,
plummeted
from
broken
hope-like
a sixty foot wall with razor wire at the top
despite
the urgency
of
every story
knife-like
to say clearly
all the
trial & tribulation
we
don't
know
smothered in
throats
labeled by
acronyms of authority & lethal force of
murderous
-like intent,
as perpetual

root cause
too
deeply hooked
to excise—
stigmatized as
our own damn fault we were born wearing a gang color,
by
percussive
dice roll
of
statistical random gunfire
& every
bigot of
racial
profile
wearing
the death
mask
of prerogative
by dint of fear

who can really know what anyone's thinking?

our
awful grace
of suffering
may be
the most human
thing
we do
always
freedom
as the Blue(s)
persist quivering &
breath-moist
on our
tongues
to numb
the
painful
bite-our-tongues

& eat
dirt
& dust of ego like overextended credit
& lion pride,
a breath
nailed
to nothing—
is small—
compared
to what?

& who can really know what anyone might do?

# I Am Trayvon Martin!

Well, what else could we do? He was hopeless. I'm no bully; I never hurt a nigger in my life. I like niggers—in their place—I know how to work 'em. But I just decided it was time a few people got put on notice. As long as I live and can do anything about it, niggers are gonna stay in their place. Niggers ain't gonna vote where I live. If they did, they'd control the government. They ain't gonna go to school with my kids. And when a nigger gets close to mentioning sex with a white woman, he's tired o' livin'. I'm likely to kill him. Me and my folks fought for this country, and we got some rights. I stood there in that shed and listened to that nigger throw that poison at me, and I just made up my mind. 'Chicago boy,' I said, 'I'm tired of 'em sending your kind down here to stir up trouble. Goddam you, I'm going to make an example of you—just so everybody can know how me and my folks stand.'
—John William "J. W." Milam, acquitted co-murderer of Emmett Till, *Look* magazine, 1956

There was just no way I could describe what was in that box. No way. And I just wanted the world to see. —Mamie Till Bradley, mother of Emmett Till, 1955


Do sacrificial angels smell of sea salt rush of tears,
snatched from sleep to sleep everlasting,
a connotation of "collateral"
                    become a label of fear,    of confrontation,

of compensation—$50, 000, $2,000—how much
does a murdered Afghan child cost         to just go away?

Euphemized like Emmett Till,
weighted down to death with 75 lb. cotton-gin fan, become
a cautionary tale for Trayvon Martin,         "Skittled" by gunshot
& weighted down to death with 115 grain, full metal jacket.
His "hoodie" complicit with fear & features darkened by the hour,
like one more plantation lullaby,
                    his cell-phone ring-tone: *You should run!!*
generations removed from an open casket like a tell-tale heart.

Geraldo thinks he brought Neighborhood Watch His/panic on himself,
wearing a "hoodie" while Black,
like driving,
        jogging,    "suspicious" saggin',
                        41 bullets inna' freeze nigger!
reaching for a wallet,    Black!

Jim Crow suspicious as
whistling at white women, Mississippi 1955,         "suspicious"
as Medger Evers in his driveway Black,    "suspicious"
as MLK at the Lorraine Motel Black,              "suspicious" as

white folks in the "hood", with guns & badges,
in my niggas' pockets
& they socks,          lookin' for some dope, or the undercover Glock.

Serious as piling 9 dead Afghan children to make a bonfire,
                under color of "Operation Enduring Freedom."

Serious as
heart attack & HIV/AIDS, the Sanford police chief,           defiant,
under color of "Stand Your Ground" racist Shock & Law.

Serious as being Black!

Serious as, nowhere in the definition of "suspicious"
is the adjective defined as a "coon"/terrorist in a gated community
wearing a "hoodie"/suicide vest, with Skittles/WMD in his pocket,

but who watches the Watchman,
                but the neglected specter of Emmett Louis Till?

**damaged goods**

her mind, a torn & tattered box
leaking foam packaging peanuts from a body stamped:
*damaged in transit* &
manhandled, adolescent trauma: beaten by the fist of it all—
life stretching her guts & ass
& hooking the anchor of her heart into something
deep & dark & treacherous.

nai/Eve: naked as the prey of Original Sin,
become passive Barbie doll, or gone ghetto Raggedy Ann—
a sackcloth shroud of fear & looking up
into betrayal's roughly fashioned dark
shadows her soul
a submissive suffering as her autobiography.

*there is nothing, but howling wind
& carrion birds*—a black & blue hollow-boned she
of torn muscle, of fight, fuck or flee,
dreading to pummel a bruised floor already veined with scars.

her conviction: assuming the blame, the buck & a belief,
now inscribed on her soul, that all men
are the brass knuckles bruising her mouth, slapped
& punched coercing her confidence to swallow
her bloodied self-esteem, black skid-marked &
passed hand to hand to hand: *do not fold, spindle or mutilate*
defacing the torn & crumpled letter (photograph enclosed)

like flyers posted in Wal-Mart exits, a second caste
that mutes her hollow plea to a mist of statistic: *have you seen me?*
that exiles her anger & shame to disappeared, like jaws agape &
slicing from the dark—
the whole of herself an offering of sacrifice
because she was born
one lone girl amongst sharks,
too scared to throw a punch, that God forbid,
might land.

**the famous-for-being-famous blues**

silver screen
          star-
ving to be
famous &
royal-titlement
in bright lights
but hate
how hungry
she looks
on screen
started
awake from
fading claw
at the end of
a roar
meth-
amphetamine dream
the oily detritus
of moral poverty
& jagged grimace
of pearly-white
ceramic caps
        give me
opulent mansions
of vogue celebrity
clawing
magnificent at the sky
lurch & dive
of sycophant &
paparazzi flashbulb
hungry for
gossip
the raptor gust &
sonic draw of
velocity
make us whom
we have to be
a kingdom to be
famous

instead of nothing
comes
to sleepers
but the dream

**stranger than fiction**

**for the celebri-hos, from Marilyn to the Kardashians**

personal ad say:

prince charming seeks submissive
virgin princess bride; Paladin: have gun, will travel; will come
on trusty steed, dragon slayer & damsel-in-distress rescuer,
White Knight, Incorporated

newspaper say:

dragon threat de-fanged of bite, but
plucky prince hideously mangled & scarred for life;
dismissed by princess via text-tweeted thanx &
dejected prince retreats to vow-of-silence monastic ranks,
cock-blocked & unrequited, one more horny recluse for life

tabloids say:

princess becomes star of sex-oriented
reality show, shakin' that booty like no tomorrow &
pussy-whups octogenarian billionaire (jackpot!)
she marries into mega-bucks

in short order, elderly hubby expires
to cardiovascular thrombosis in coitus flagrante;
the fans a-tweet to her red carpet show of grief:
trophy wife dons mourning mantle—black veil &
little black mini-dress by Oscar de la Renta—
*i really & truly loved him . . . to death did we part*

sexpot inherits socialite status & opulent palace, as groupies twitter
sympathetic oooohs & aaahhs, but too soon succumbs
to bath tub o. d. by prescription drugs, a televised
celebrity interment & immortalized post-mortem: one more celebri-ho,
*famous for being famous*

breaking news say:

the butler did it!
bold, front-page expose: *i'm the father of the princess's daughter*
as sharks in Armani circle the scandal of the month &
file court orders in-between double martini lunch

## comeuppance: the self-serving

no pain of death
measures up to
one been stripped
of dignity
to one been discrimin-
ated against
said the black man lynched
cynically

i used to
bring my children here
post-amber alert . . .
but how do you read
the flashing sign on the freeway
if you're on your
cell-phone?
asked the tortured &
raped eight-year old
with a smirk

the definition of a fool: you did not
have the courage or common sense
to take a stand
against the patriot act
realized the frequent flyer
sales rep
who was dragged from the plane &
arrested
for texting a muslim

**the salvage blues**

**salvage** */sálvij/ • n.* **1 rescue of property, from the sea, fire, etc.**
 **3b *v.tr.*  save from a wreck, fire, adverse circumstances, etc.**
   **—The Oxford American Desk Dictionary and Thesaurus, 2nd ed.**

salvage:
a ghost of a man inna cardboard box,
fetus-posed, lookin' like hell sued for murder,
emptied Thunderbird inna' crumpled paper sack—

a victory of the echo over the voice:
they show you what you aren't,
then show you what you're supposed to be,

a punishment made real
by a drought of unattained dreams & foreclosure
on one more last chance

salvage:
the slow erosion of hope
& perseverance,
abandoning life to a monotonous irony
that becomes morbid to the recycled—

what they say & do when you are lost is how you are finally found,

reborn without prior knowledge of self
is the irony that lies at the nexus of the myth of hell;
there is no serendipity in reclamation,

a frozen wail of righteous heresy,
distended air-sandwich belly heaving
one last "fuck-you-God!"
holding on till help come along

salvage:
burning & burial
that collapses everything
into memory,
something destroyed, abandoned
or cast aside,

as in, he tried to salvage their marriage;
see what i mean?
or, she tried to salvage her relationship with her estranged daughter
that highlights the inadequacy of "i'm sorry"

salvage:
rejected hearts shattered
into pieces too onerous to curl up
& die—

broken by betrayal into spiteful conniption fits

salvage:
as in, an addiction,
a desperate repetition of previous failure:
flight to avoid prosecution, with purpose

salvage:
resuscitate,

as in, petro-rems of plastic twisted into kilo-tons of strangle

not unlike a surgical, military strike, a boom-boom-booming
that leaves whoever suffered, or died, a mystery defined by euphemism

salvage:
recycled for the eye of the beholder
as in, front page news:
"BP Engineers Prepare For Next Bid to Stop Oil Flow"

**Note:** Rescue does not infer salvation. One can be rescued from a fire, but still remain doomed by the third degree burns covering 90 percent of the body.
 Salvage, on the other hand—as in save or salvation—distinctly covers a precise application of deliverance. One's soul can be saved, thus eliminating the need for bottled water in Hell, or one can be salvaged from a brutal relationship by eliminating the aggressor with a few surgically implanted bullets—problem solved.
 Whereas rescue can leave one precariously positioned on the periphery of danger, salvage removes the victim from, or away from, the debilitating persistence of danger. For example, giving advice is one fish that quells immediate hunger, unlike extending the helping hand of empathy, teaching the needy to fish, thus eliminating their hunger for life. The deliberately compassionate action of saving precludes the ego-enhancing pronouncement of rescue.

# SEPT. 11:
## cheney's puppet seizes 31ˢᵗ piece of silver

**Man is born free, but everywhere he is in chains.**
**—Jean-Jacques Rousseau**

two parallel blue beams of light
pierce the new york city skyline
reminding the world of the right way to tell a lie

after the planes
flames & death & concrete dust tsunami

we looked the other way
from gotham twin temples to "shock & awe"

935 guv'ment lies & collusion put to sleep, tucked in
with false platitudes of sound-bite grief
& happily-ever-after war on terrorism

a blues-toned laughter of corporate patriotism
pulling the wings from foreign lives, a collateral damage
sealing our moment of snail's determination

more fallen towers & mass destruction . . .

hiroshima     nagasaki     bosnia     afghanistan
el salvador     somalia     viet nam
grenada     bagdad     nicaragua     & pakistan

the incorrigible korea     & maybe soon  tehran?
that portends the tainted beauty & child-like atrocity
of democracy . . .

the high & mighty almighty sequestered
out of sight & out of mind
as agony sifted the rubble in search of blame

new york new york
asphalt, concrete, glass & steel
reality interred beneath a rubbl-ized scar of greed

become stillborn propaganda  toxic to breathe
become a fading whore whose eyes have seen too much

meditation pool
(coming soon!)

# Eve #2

Eve was the color that surprised Him
after the Mississippi red dirt & debris
of Adam, after
the aggressive indigo to ephemeral foam
of ocean,
the azure, forever & ever, dome of sky.

Eve, all phoenix fire-red &
golden immolation,
daylight
risen from the mutiny of Lilith,
her willfulness,
the first person of disobedience:
*My apple . . . because . . . I want it.*

**broke-ass blues**

Always what is & what was longed for,

  folded inwards upon reflection, as if
  he could subtract his losses & turn back the hands of time.

  He sang, blood-bucket rhythms of consequence:
  shattered whiskey bottle & crushed pack of Camels,

  dead roach spattered with after-hours sweat, hinting at
  something humorous, as well as, trial & tribulation.

  He sang about the darker current we ride, & always,
  the blues ain't gonna make you cry:

Testing & backstabbing,
  & pulling the knife out to lick our wounds & try to heal,

  only to make a scar
  that says: *Stab Here, Repeatedly.*

  He sang, in a gravel-
  throated growl: *you cain't spend what you ain't got &*

  *you cain't lose what you ain't never had—*
  the pain made palatable,

  but lingering,
  like a southern vowel drawn out of itself.

  He sang, a lament-like
  warning—treading carefully around shards of broken glass,

  beginnings & endings in green bottleneck riffs—bitch & moan
  walking forty years across the desert waiting for a sign

  & always, ten feet tall & bulletproof,

  the gut-bucket blues ain't no monkey-junk!
  poured into song halfway between hope & nowhere soon:

the crossroad-dirt color of almost in the sound of a moan,
the mojo-workin' hope of maybe, like *We Shall Overcome.*

Knife-cuttin' guitar chords &
cotton-field holla'

jook-joint signifyin' from sun-down to sun-up—
something about hellhounds, fast Cadillac

women & broken hearts—bad luck & trouble—
something about unrequited love

                                    from a whiskey-broken tongue.

**Chance is what's left, when you've run out of hope.**

 How does He choose *who*
 gets how much?
The distant gaze of omnipotence before
 the slapdash assumption of choice.
As if appraised by predator suddenly
  rising
 from tall grass.
To assess opportunity?    To measure
 the handicap of the expendable gimp?

 & with the capricious certainty of
 suffering      famine with drought
 the homeless without   the uniformed
 schoolgirl & raincoat stranger
                           with sweets
 we wonder: Does God
 allow only a finite amount of pain
 in the world?   How does He choose?
To take it from one place &
 leave it as careless litter in another?

**synonym the low bass quiver**

a darkness.　living life for the sake of life.
desperate
for meaning pregnant with
light.　a tribulation moment &
　　　then gone.　& from
　　　that darkness.　in spite of
　　　　　　　not enough oxygen.
　　　　　　　become DNA hemorrhage
　　　　　　　that eviscerate the narrative
　　　　　　　to something worn as
　　　　armor.
　　　　　　　the gift of labor.
the gift of song & story.
　　　　　　the gift of Spirit.
　　　　　　the gift of struggle.　of constant sorrow.
all hardcore muthafuckas
　　　　are manufactured
　　　malleable.　can hide
　　　　　　the insecurity of blackness
　　　　　　like a razor
　　　　　　inside a roll
　　of big-head hundreds.
　　　　　　　　　signifyin'
　　　　　　　　　*tense-*
　　　　　　　　　*coiled*
　　　　　　　　　shadow dialect.　　tha' dozens
　flaunting trademark sneakers.　can synonym the low bass quiver.
　　　　　　　the heavy breath
　　　　　　　rumble youngblood rumble bass in gut &
　　　　　　　blunt
　　　　　　　radioactive fists of
　funkadelic cosmic molecules.
　　　　　　　　　is get-the-Holy Ghost gospel.
　　　　　a new depiction
　of blackfolk.
　　　　　　the sliver of chicken bone
　　　　　　come home to roost　　looming
　　　　　　　　　the reckoning to come.

# El-Hajj Malik El-Shabazz

*1. The Lost Years*

The soon-lion began, was Malcolm Little once, the man-child soon
zoot-suit hustler & thief,
soon Detroit Red
snared in the U.S. of Penitentiary, like 90 goin' north of freedom,
east of where his murdered father
                                once sermonized the Black Train Homeward.

An incremental stealth
*stranded in a hungerland of great prosperity*, like every black man
who stores his hope in an unsure place—always looking for something better
than Made in Amerikkka—aware

of that which is most dangerous, of duplicity, of that which
is to be withheld & granted selectively: language
that says one thing & means
                        an entirely other.

He lion wait
where the freedman
fades causality,
with courage spitting bullets,
as complex as
revolution with the swagger of conviction,
as willful as
*by any means necessary*.

*2. Up, you mighty race; you can accomplish what you will!*

The dignity of the idea, invisible, but undiminished,
our jazz & our slang—coalescing holy dervish of the inner-city blues
faced with the transparency of the outside gaze & fragmented
into component blacknesses:

Minor Al Capone in the U.S. of Negro.    Prisoner no. 22843,
compressing the moan that becomes a cry that shines forth faceted light,
like a tribe of hammers striking railroad spikes

because we remembered
                        that we could.

*He rose, renewed, renamed became*
*much more than there was time for him to be:* Orator supreme
reborn X of black vernacular & conjugated defiant while black.

3. *What are the roots that clutch, what branches grow*
   *Out of this stony rubbish?*

First minister of the Lost-Found Nation of Islam,
rising from the belly of the beast, from the mist of segregation per Elijah,
fleshing out our dreams of freedom from the hate that made hate—
                        an incandescent glare that purges what was love—
*this liberty, this beautiful & terrible thing, this needful to man as air.*

Testing fate between gravity & Allah, between how much pressure
to make a diamond, between each word a logical Word spoken as truth,
as more militant metaphor, like lion-like brave &
unafraid,
like why delay anger
that must rage & exclaim & grow ancient?
Like a voiceless, massing maelstrom of moths
seeking out our own burning, as needs must
                        when the devil drives.

I've seen a man drown in an inch of determination,
a love of self wielding the eventuality of a force greater than our weaknesses.

I've seen a man
wrecked in noon but having ridden the eddies of the sun, buried alive,
neck-deep in what only he perceives & passionately dreaming
the Black Train Homeward; the messiah, betrayed with a kiss. . .
                        *our manhood, our living, black manhood*
into the redeeming pressure of Allah & carrying the scent of things
                        lost in the fire.

**Note:** incorporated into this poem are italicized fragments by June Jordan (2nd stanza),
    Robert Hayden (7th & 8th stanza), T.S. Eliot (3rd subtitle) & Ossie Davis (10th stanza)

## waste is everything nobody needs

1.

the aerodynamic glare of light that shimmers across water,
a flaunted beauty,
skating through air as silvered glints in the voice of purpose,
a silent need, hewn, as if from ripples in the river, or
false reflections mimicking neural traffic, sometimes wisp,
sometimes, ponderous as planets.

2.

flags of revolutionary weeds origami-unfolding
from cracks & crannies,
rising from a calligraphy of capricious cleavage
with the fragile silence of eyes rolled back in pain—

3.

pain, written in blood squeezed from nowhere,
& less than zero, exploited in the crawl space of excess, the ease
with which one can be undone, the randomness of flipped coins,
like the powerless squat downstairs, peeling scabs
from wounds of circumstance.

4.

is there a somewhere for everything,
some terrible sealed lip stealing silence from itself?

**fade to black**

i come from a place where people are judged by what we see,
the gap between words, the innuendo after ellipse—
what they got, or ain't got . . . who someone said they were,
instead of whom they really are—

where inhumane justification punctuates human nature,
ever plagued by shadows of regret,

by corporate caste creeping across the mind, as intolerance
fingers the deadbolt securing the door of tribe mentality;

fear by assumption ripples across the face
in those first-impression moments, securing the eventuality
of deferred dreams, foreshadowed, like a cubist menagerie
run amok:

a vertical line of dignity obscured by shame, a horizontal slash
of despair splashed bloody over an obtuse angle of blind hope

& minds are forged, molten to annealed to hardened, or obliterated,
into a brief dark night of remaining days,
into decaying increments of sustained silence suspended
like a season of strange fruit.

# ACKNOWLEDGMENTS

Many thanks to the editors of the following journals in which these poems—sometimes in earlier versions—first appeared.

1. "red" in *The Write Room*; *Poised in Flight* (Anthology); *Scissors & Spackle*; *Storm Cycle, 2013 Best of Anthology*

2. "match & gasoline blues" in *Generations Literary Journal*

3. "selective recall" in *Upstairs in The Library* (Anthology); *hardpan: a journal of poetry*; *Blue Moon Literary & Art Review*; *Tic Toc* (Anthology)

4. "Sigourney Valentine O'Connell, aka Muse" in *Rufous City Review*

5. "seven days in oz" in *hardpan: a journal of poetry*

6. "dissent relegated to the annuls of history" in *BlazeVox*

7. "the terminal blues" in *TicToc* (Anthology)

8. "tradition" in *Blue Lake Review*

9. "bitter margins" in *Suisun Valley Review*

10. "the price of flight" in *Subliminal Interiors Literary Arts Magazine*; *Poised in Flight* (Anthology); featured on *bulatag.wordpress.com*

11. "The Lion Pauses" in *Blue Lake Review*; *EWR: Everyday Poetry*; *Penny Ante Feud*

12. "allotment" in *Suisun Valley Review*

13. "the soul would have no rainbow if eyes had no tears" in *Blue Moon Literary & Art Review*

14. "Requiem for Eve: A Whiter Shade of Pale in Five Parts" in *Subliminal Interiors Literary Arts Magazine*; *The Write Room*

15. "I Am Trayvon Martin!" in *BlazeVox*; *Empirical Magazine*

16. "damaged goods" in *Soul Vomit* (Anthology)

17. "stranger than fiction" in *Nameless Magazine*

18. "the salvage blues" in *BlazeVox*

19. "Eve #2" in *Black Heart Magazine*

20. "El-Hajj Malik El-Shabazz" in *Dead Flowers: A Poetry Rag; Mandala Literary Journal*

## *About the Author*

henry 7. reneau, jr.

writes words in fire to wake the world ablaze & illuminated by courage that empathizes with all the awful moments: a freight train bearing down with warning that blazes from the heart, like a chambered bullet exploding inadvertently.

now,    runantellyomamaboutdat!!

www.ingramcontent.com/pod-product-compliance
Lightning Source LLC
Chambersburg PA
CBHW070326100426
42743CB00011B/2580